START YOUR OWN SENIOR HOME CARE BUSINESS

THE COMPLETE GUIDE TO STARTING A PROFITABLE SENIOR HOME CARE BUSINESS

MARK SANDERS

TABLE OF CONTENTS

TABLE OF CONTENTS

INTRODUCTION

While we are occupied with living our carries on with every day, working, raising our kids, enjoying our family, we never think about it about who will deal with us in our retirement years when the requirement for care emerges. Nobody stops to think about this issue despite the fact that we have as long as we can remember to get ready. Until a loved one abruptly has a crisis, an unanticipated disease, or injury, this theme does not enter our mind. Families today are confronted with the test of providing care for their loved ones every day.

What is more, truly, we basically cannot stop the clock, and for most seniors, there will come when some additional help performing the assignments of day by day living would be useful. The Home Care Association of America reports that "almost 70% of Americans who arrive at 65 will be not able to care for themselves eventually without help." For certain individuals, this help implies moving into an assisted living office or a nursing home, yet for some, more, "aging set up" at home is a considerably more appealing objective that can be accomplished with the assistance of senior home care.

America is aging quick. There are presently very nearly 50 million senior residents more than 65 in the U.S, and that number is required to twofold in only a couple of years. As seniors age, particularly in their 70s and 80s, they need more assistance at home doing undertakings most more youthful people underestimate, which implies a growing requirement for a senior home care business in each network, enormous or little.

On account of their age and medical problems, numerous seniors are homebound or less portable, and need a touch of help at home with a portion of the routine assignments that used to be so natural for them, similar to feast arrangement, light housekeeping, shopping and tasks. As meager as two hours per day of help can have a major effect enabling seniors to remain in their own homes which is the thing that 90% of them need. At home, they have natural surroundings, security and independence.

In light of this senior populace boom, the interest for senior services has developed quickly to keep pace. A standout amongst other senior service businesses is a senior home care business. It is a productive and satisfying approach to help other people and take in substantial income doing it. On the off chance that you are curious about it, you may have a few inquiries before you are prepared to begin.

However, as youngsters we have to recall that our folks consistently gave the best care to us. As youthful adults on our approach to begin our own lives, we have to recollect that our folks financially dealt with us too. As adults with our own families, let us furnish them with a similar thought in their requirement for quality care. They were consistently there for us, in the midst of hardship. Presently, we ought to be there for them. Do not they merit the best?

When you have sorted out your needs, the time has come to assess which home care services are appropriate for you and where to find the best providers. Obviously, it very well may be hard to endow your home or individual care to other people, particularly individuals you do not have the foggiest idea. Regardless of whether you draw in a home care service provider legitimately or work through an agency, you can mollify your feelings of dread by conducting some fundamental examination.

Moreover, start by seeking referrals from family, companions, or neighbors. There might be a neighbor who could routinely registration with you or give yard maintenance, for instance;

Neighborhood strict gatherings now and again offer suppers or social exercises for seniors. Ask the individuals you know whether they have care providers they can suggest. Your Doctor or other healthcare expert may likewise have the option to give referrals.

Full-service agencies ordinarily come at a greater expense yet give prescreened candidates who have just had individual verifications. Since the caregiver works for the agency, they deal with billing and expense issues. They may likewise be fortified for issues, for example, robbery. In the event that a caregiver stops or is not working out, an agency can generally find a substitution rapidly, and may likewise give inclusion if a caregiver phones in debilitated.

Independent providers generally come at a lower cost, yet require more legwork on your part. You should deal with any assessment necessities and perform personal investigations and character check. For the situation of sickness or unexpected termination, you will likewise be answerable for finding a substitution provider.

Why You Should Start A Seniors Home Care Business

It very well may be frightening and painful to see somebody you love struggling to care for themselves. Maybe you have seen that your loved one's home has gotten a lot messier than it used to be, or that they are wearing stained, messy garments. Possibly unmistakably they have not had a shower for some time, or when you open the cooler, there is not really any food inside. Or on the other hand maybe your loved one has endured an ongoing fall or you have seen a container burning unattended on the oven.

Now and again, declines can happen progressively or an unexpected change in wellbeing or a critical misfortune can trigger issues. Whatever the explanation, in the event that you are stressed over a loved one's wellbeing or the state of their home, it is critical to propose the topic carefully.

Express your interests as your own, without accusing - A more seasoned loved one may be more open to your legitimate articulations of concern. For instance, instead of saying "It is clear you cannot deal with yourself any longer. Something should be done," attempt "I have truly been stressed over you. It harms me to think that you probably will not get everything you need. What do you think we ought to do?"

Regard your loved one's self-rule and involve them in choices -Except if your loved one is incapacitated, the final choice about care is up to them. You can help by offering recommendations and thoughts for home care services. On the off chance that you are concerned that home care probably will not be sufficient, what different choices are accessible? You can outline it as something to attempt briefly instead of trying to force a lasting arrangement.

Attempt to find the genuine purposes for any opposition - A loved one who is impervious to receiving help could be terrified that they are not, at this point ready to do errands that were once in the past so natural. It may be more agreeable to deny it and minimize any issues. Maybe they are grieving the departure of a loved one, or baffled at not being ready to interface with companions as effectively as they once did. Or on the other hand possibly they are awkward with having outcasts in their home.

Enroll the assistance of others - Does your loved one know other people who have utilized home care services? Talking to other people who have had positive encounters can now and again assist eliminate with fearing of the obscure. Some of the time hearing input from a fair outsider, for example, a specialist or geriatric care chief, can enable a loved one to understand that things need to change.

Definitively, starting and owning a senior home care is a decent business investment with individual or government funding, is useful for the network and gives a choice to assisted living, nursing homes and other wellbeing related institutions.

CHAPTER - 1

WHAT IS SENIOR HOME CARE?

(TYPICAL NON - MEDICAL SERVICES)

What are Senior Homecare Services?

Senior home care services are the ideal choice for seniors who need to remain in their own homes, yet need help to do as such. According to AARP, 90% of seniors beyond 65 years old intend to remain in their own homes as they age.

Before you begin determining what sort of care is ideal for you, it is fundamental that you have an understanding of what your various choices are.

Is it becoming harder to maintain your home? Do you want to deal with your own prescription, cleanliness, family unit tasks, suppers, and more has gotten overwhelming?

Maybe you have an inclination that you have arrived at the point where you are not, at this point ready to remain in your own home. In the event that you are a senior and you are facing these difficulties, you may feel like you just have two alternatives for your living game plans: possibly you move into an assisted living network or you move in with a relative who can care for you. Albeit assisted living is another famous choice for seniors, this is not generally the correct decision for each senior. You may not feel that you are prepared to leave your home and move into a network. A couple of downsides of moving into an assisted living network include the high month to month cost and the absence of room for your assets.

Luckily, there is another alternative you ought to consider. You can remain in your own home and get the normal care and backing you need. Senior homecare services permit seniors who are not, at this point capable or find it challenging to live alone to remain in their own home, where they feel great. All things considered, you may have lived in your home for quite a long time, and on the grounds that it is truly significant that you never penance security for comfort, this could be the most ideal approach to have a sense of security and agreeable.

All in all, what precisely is senior homecare? Basically, a gifted healthcare provider comes to you to offer the help you need to get past the day. These expert caregivers assisted with various parts of everyday living. Homecare services are custom fitted to whatever you need, regardless of whether that is a ride to your next medical checkup or somebody to stroll with you in the recreation center. Every day, enthusiastic, and medical help are at the essence of what homecare providers offer.

While a lot of senior home care is centered around enabling seniors to remain in their own homes, homecare service providers are not limited to simply in-home care. Homecare services can be offered any place your home might be, regardless of whether that is a brief or perpetual home. A care proficient can help in a recovery office, providing friendship and extra help, or in an assisted living office on the off chance that you have an inclination that you are not getting enough quality care or consideration, or on the off chance that you essentially need a buddy.

This is particularly valuable for seniors who move in with their kids or other relatives. Moving in with your family does not naturally mean somebody will be accessible to give you care and backing during the day. Perhaps your youngsters work all day or your grandkids are at school. Senior homecare services imply that somebody is accessible to help you, regardless of whether your family is not home.

Characteristics That Make Senior Homecare Providers Stand Out

You have gauged your choices and concluded that in-home healthcare is the best strategy for your loved one. It does not expect them to be removed yet instead permits them to get similar quality healthcare from the solaces of their own home. While making the choice to pick in-home healthcare rather than a live-in office may have been simple, presently comes the crucial step choosing from the numerous senior homecare services in around the globe. The alternatives might be many, however that does not really imply that they are on the whole great decisions. Those healthcare providers that offer predominant in-home medical care have a couple of key characteristics that will separate them from the rest.

- **Qualifications**

Regardless of which in-home service you select, confirm their certifications before proceeding. Every foundation ought to be authorized with the state. They ought to have the option to show you a printed version of their business permit and it should at present be substantial. On head of that, confirm that your picked provider is likewise reinforced, meaning that their services are insured. Should any of your planned in-home healthcare providers be lacking one of these confirmations, look somewhere else.

On head of the genuine agency being guaranteed, it is significant that every one of their caregivers is additionally appropriately taught. Every individual that cares for your loved one ought to either be a doctor, Certified Nurse's Assistant (CNA), Registered Nurse (RN), or a Home Health Aid (HHA). This guarantees that they have gotten sufficient training to administer the medicines expected to your loved one.

Smiling caregiver embracing glad senior lady in nursing home

- **Devotion**

Caring for elderly patients can be trying. On head of dealing with various sicknesses and juggling multi-faceted care, in-home wellbeing providers additionally need to deal with the desires for the family they are working for. It takes a significant level of pledge to guarantee that care is administered expertly. The service that you pick ought to be conscious of your loved one and your family. They will not deny care or withdrawal services immediately. Instead, they will remain faithful and committed to the circumstance, showing up when required.

- **Innovativeness**

Great in-home providers are continually looking for better approaches to inspire their patients. Seniors, particularly, can get stuck in a psychological groove as they age. Because of their wellbeing limitations or physical impediments, they may not feel that they have such a personal satisfaction. The correct healthcare provider will introduce new exercises to assist seniors with regaining the pizzazz that they may have lost. Seniors will learn new aptitudes, improve their independence, and gain comfort in their own capacity to complete different errands.

- **Basic Thinking and Judgment**

While your in-home healthcare provider may likewise perform light housekeeping and cooking, they are there for one main reason to give quality healthcare. This is not in every case simple to do, however. Since your loved one is not residing in an office or being treated in a clinic, it is regularly important to take care of issues on the spot. Your healthcare service ought to have the option to practice trustworthiness and settle on essential choices with regards to the wellbeing of your loved one. Regardless of whether it is an adjustment in dose or an increase in physical movement, these sorts of choices ought to be made informatively as they could affect their patient's wellbeing.

- **Bedside Manner**

Your loved one is presumably previously feeling somewhat vulnerable. Those assignments that were once simple to perform are currently additionally challenging. They may feel like they have lost their independence or that life has no meaning. Regardless of how they are feeling, the correct home healthcare service can either help or hurt the circumstance. With a positive and humane disposition, your healthcare provider can be a beam of sunshine in the life of your loved one. Search for those services that value their bedside way. It is not just about improving the wellbeing of patient; it is tied in with inspiring and providing would like to those out of luck.

A solid home care service will help the weight of your family and give a reestablished plan to your loved one.

When are Homecare Services Helpful?

Homecare services can be on an impermanent or lasting premise. While you might be needing help now, you may not later on. Here are a couple of life occasions that may trigger the requirement for senior homecare services:

Recovering from an Illness or Injury - Have you as of late encountered a disease or injury and you need assistance while you recuperate? Possibly after a stay in the clinic, you do not have as much quality as did before your stay. A fall, similar to a disease, can likewise make it much harder to satisfy your normal duties and care for yourself. Homecare services can help you incidentally recoup from these difficulties, or they can oblige you in the event that you need help long haul to recuperate from an injury or ailment. Recollect that injuries or ailments can be more diligently to conquer the more seasoned you get, so it is significant you have upheld as you recuperate.

Managing a Chronic or Permanent Condition - Chronic sickness or the conclusion of a perpetual condition like Alzheimer's illness or diabetes will transform you.

Shockingly, with another analysis regularly comes new difficulties, and there is an opportunity you will not, at this point have the option to do things that used to be simple. In that situation, homecare services can take a portion of these weights off your shoulders or minimize the measure of care relatives need to give. Notwithstanding broad care needs, a caregiver can likewise assist you with managing your prescriptions, some of which may have been as of late endorsed, ensuring you take the perfect meds at the perfect time every day.

Help with Daily Tasks - Sometimes seniors arrive at the point where they are not, at this point capable or no longer need to stay aware of certain errands all alone. Having somebody there to offer help with day by day errands is one of the most widely recognized reasons seniors search out homecare services.

Life partner Recently Passed Away - The passing of a companion is devastating. Regardless of whether they were the caregiver for you or you were the caregiver for them, you presently need to restore as long as you can remember. An in-home caregiver furnishes help as you think of another routine and arrange your loved one's belongings. They are an incredible wellspring of general care and friendship during this trying time.

Perpetual Caregiver is Unavailable - Maybe you have a lasting caregiver, similar to a companion or a kid. Here and there, the person may not be accessible because of conditions like an excursion, jury obligation, or an ailment they are dealing with themselves. At the point when they are not accessible, a caregiver can step in to fill that job. Scheduling homecare services does not need to be a perpetual course of action. Actually, you could have fill-in care for stints as short as one day.

Facing the End of Life - In the final period of life, you may require uphold both genuinely and strategically. There is extraordinary solace in having a healthcare proficient focused on helping you. Preparing for a mind-blowing finish is a daunting errand, and one that needs help both for you and your loved ones. A homecare expert can help seniors nearing the finish of their lives get things in request or help oversee pain to make this season agreeable and tranquil.

On the off chance that you find yourself in any of these situations, do not stress. There are help choices accessible. Homecare services are intended to offer the help you need, when you need it, in the way that is generally agreeable for you. Furthermore, when you have enough recouped from a medical procedure or a sickness is behind you, you can stop care visits until you need them again, or on the off chance that you need these services consistently, caregivers are accessible for long haul uphold, as well.

What Types of Homecare Services are Available?

The response to this inquiry is truly basic: caregivers can offer help with nearly anything you need! The objective of homecare services is essentially to offer whatever help a senior need to live an agreeable, glad, and sound life. In this way, the services required will presumably appear to be somewhat unique for each senior.

Homecare services fall into two general classifications – individual care services, and friendship and homemaking services. Let us take a gander at some particular services that fall into these two classifications.

A. Individual Care Services

- **Bathing**

Bathing can be a fall risk for seniors, particularly on the off chance that you do not have a debilitation available bathroom in your home. A few seniors need help to securely get in and out of the shower or bath, or washing their hair and body. Homecare services guarantee you can wash securely.

- **Grooming**

Getting dressed, shaving, or doing your hair would all be able to be draining undertakings without the assistance of a homecare service provider. Be that as it may, with the assistance of a caregiver, you can look and feel your best every day.

- **Cleanliness**

Individual cleanliness is significant, yet keeping up with basic regular undertakings, such as brushing your teeth or cutting fingernails and toenails, can be a test without help. Homecare providers can deal with these little assignments effortlessly.

• **Toileting**

On the off chance that you do not have a debilitation open bathroom or bathroom frill, your wellbeing could be in danger. Also, regardless of whether you do have these offices, help might be required. Try not to hazard a fall. The help of a caregiver can assist you with avoiding genuine injury.

• **Incontinence**

Homecare experts can help address all incontinence issues, helping you maintain wellbeing and nobility.

B. Friendship and House-Making Services

• **Dinner Preparation**

For some, seniors, preparing food can be debilitating to the point that they may skip suppers or pick undesirable alternatives over solid ones. Healthcare providers do not simply make dinner planning simpler for you, they additionally uphold you in staying sound.

- **Transportation**

Numerous seniors do not feel great driving any longer, yet at the same time have a lot of spots to go. On the off chance that you need somebody to take you to regular checkups or to reorder your medicines, homecare services could be the appropriate response.

- **Tasks**

Notwithstanding transportation for appointments, homecare experts can likewise assist you with running vital tasks, such as picking up staple goods or meeting companions for lunch.

Instead of being confined to your home or relying on a relative to get your things done, you can appreciate break of the house with a caregiver and scratch these undertakings off your plan for the day.

- **Housekeeping**

Maintaining a spotless home is a test at any age, however it tends to be particularly trying for seniors. Scrubbing the bath or kitchen floor is absurd or savvy.

Homecare services can help with basic assignments like tidying up, washing or folding clothing, doing dishes, or some other errand you cannot do.

- **Friendship**

Numerous seniors battle with loneliness. Restricted versatility, awful climate, or ailment would all be able to disrupt the general flow of associations with companions or family. A homecare service proficient can assist you with overcoming the test of loneliness. While this service is two hours overall, the measure of time is truly up to you. You can have a homecare service provider remain as long as you need.

- **Drug Reminders**

In the event that you take different prescriptions, you realize how challenging it tends to be to stay aware of which medicines to take at what time. Besides, taking an inappropriate prescription or an inappropriate measurement can have genuine ramifications for your wellbeing. Medicine the board from a homecare proficient is not only a helpful service. It is a service that advances your wellbeing and security.

- **Pet Services**

A pet can bring enormous euphoria and friendship regardless of your age, however the more seasoned you get, the harder it tends to be to play with, walk, and tidy up after a pet. Senior homecare experts can contribute with pet care, helping you walk your canine or take you and your feline to the vet. That way you do not need to forfeit advantage of a pet because old enough or capacity.

As you take a gander at these services, remember that the ideal opportunity for each undertaking can change. Possibly your tasks will just take 30 minutes, or you need not bother with assistance with grooming by any stretch of the imagination. The advantage of using the care-by-the-minute structure is that you just compensation for the services you need, and you just compensation for the measure of time you need them.

CHAPTER - 2

SETTING UP YOUR SENIOR HOME CARE BUSINESS

Tips for Setting Up Your Own (Non-Medical) Senior Home Care Business

Starting a senior care business, for example, a non-medical home care business, is an ideal method to gain a strong income while helping seniors remain in their own homes to the extent that this would be possible. As the expense of senior housing, for example, senior care networks and assisted-living offices, continues to increase, staying put is a reasonable alternative. Also, more than 90% of seniors state they want to age set up instead of leave their home.

Caring for seniors in their own homes is a basic business that permits caregivers to work for themselves and work the hours they like. There are a few things you should know before you start a senior care business that will get you looking smooth so far. Specifically, here are some tips that are particularly significant:

- **Make a business plan**

This is the initial phase in starting any sort of business. You have to make a business arrangement for your home care business since it is the base of your organization and will be required for each progression to follow. A business plan includes the following:

- Leader rundown – Explain the nuts and bolts of your organization.

- Organization portrayal – Write the mission and objectives of your home medical services agency.

- Services – Describe what services you will give.

- Marketing plan – How will individuals find out about your business? Choose the pricing of your business too.

- The board and association – Describe the possession structure of your home care business.

- Operational arrangement – Explain the office and staff, just as provisions you should work.

- Financial arrangement – This is the place you will compose an income projection, monetary record depiction and equal the initial investment examination.

- ## Licensing a non-medical home care business

A non-medical senior home care business is a lot simpler to begin than a home medical care business, since it does not ordinarily need authorized medical caregivers, for example, attendants. Along these lines, not all states have licensing and enrollment necessities for a non-medical care business. Before you do anything else, check with your state or city licensing office to find what their particular guidelines are for home care services.

- ## Insurance

You will require insurance for your non-medical home care business. In the event that you drive a client's vehicle or utilize your own vehicle to ship clients or their pets, you will require inclusion for that. Likewise, on the off chance that you do house-sit or pet-sitting for clients, you will require the inclusion of "care, custody and control." Check with your insurance specialist or an insurance intermediary to realize what is suggested for your home care business.

- ## Supplies for your home care business

You will not need a ton of provisions to begin a fruitful non-medical home care business, however there are a couple of basics. Most importantly, you will require a dependable vehicle to drive you to and from your positions, and a phone to keep in contact with your customers. Practically any cell phone will do, and you can likewise utilize it to monitor your timetable and the hours you work for every client.

Next, it is a smart thought to have business cards printed and maybe an attractive sign for your vehicle. You can purchase both online to set aside cash. Both the cards and the attractive signs are accessible at sensible cost. Having these will make attention to your new business, and remind possibilities to call you for their home care needs.

- **Legitimate structure for your senior home-care business**

There are a couple of things you should do to arrangement your new non-medical home care business legitimately. Most importantly, settle on the lawful structure of your business. Will you be a sole owner, an organization or an LLC? This will determine what charges you pay, and how you document your assessment forms.

- **Register with the state**

You should incorporate your business, get your assessment ID and register for your NPI (National Provider Identification) number. An EIN is like your SSN with the IRS and is utilized to recognize your organization for charge obligation.

An NPI is an extraordinary recognizable proof number that is allocated to distinguish secured home care providers.

These prerequisites for starting a home care business rely upon a state-to-state premise.

Likewise, when you have chosen your business name, check accessibility for the name you have decided for your business with the state.

Make certain to remember the domain name you will buy for your site when deciding your business name.

After your name has been affirmed, begin on having your agency's business cards, pamphlets and letterheads printed to mirror your new image.

- **Business Entity Identification**

- Sole owner

- Association

- Restricted Liability Company (LLC)

- S company

- C company

• Pick services to offer

Making a rundown of the services you intend to offer is a fundamental initial step, so you have to think about what might be required and what is popular in your general vicinity. A few people represent considerable authority in break care, others appreciate housekeeping, and others love to get things done. Ask other senior care providers what services are generally required in your town. At the point when you are done, make up a rundown that can be an aspect of your flyer or leaflet, or an ad on a site. It is a smart thought to include this toward the finish of the rundown. This permits you to ensure you are meeting the requirements of all your imminent clients, as you will undoubtedly miss a couple popular services when you make up that rundown.

• Name your home care business

Presently you are prepared to name your senior home care business. Think of something snappy and significant. Models include: "Senior Helpers," "Loving Caregivers," and "Eldercare Angels." Consider adding the name of your town, or even your own name, in the business name. Check with your state to ensure nobody else is using your name, and that it has not been enrolled or reserved as of now.

Now and again you may even feel overpowered as well as circumstances can get difficult. It is imperative to require some investment and ponder the reasons why you began your home care business in the beginning. Submerge yourself in the little achievements en route and recall that your agency has become that adjustment in somebody's life through your will to begin a business that shares your empathy and care for other people.

CHAPTER - 3

FINDING YOUR CUSTOMERS

The achievement of your home care business relies upon building your client base by seeking out new referral sources in your locale. Sound home care agencies comprehend the gigantic preferred position of learning innovative plans to find families that are needing your services. As proprietor, administrator, or marketing illustrative of your home care business, execute a portion of the following commonsense procedures to secure significant client referrals.

Approaches to Get New Home Care Customers

1. Start volunteering at nearby wellbeing fairs, school work out schedules, blood drives, clothing gift focuses, soup kitchens and other network supported causes.

Convey through ongoing volunteer endeavors that sympathy and trust are the establishment of your business.

2. Speak at nearby senior habitats, senior lofts, and retirement networks. Select interesting points on solid aging, for example, sustenance, exercise, sexuality, and memory improvement.

3. Be a visitor speaker at assisted living offices, nursing or recovery offices to meet inhabitants that might be needing extra close to home and steady care services not as of now gave.

4. Join neighborhood, state and public home care associations and seek after accreditations that exhibit your business' pledge to quality care. Advance your accomplishments in the neighborhood media to fabricate your notoriety in the network.

5. Start a caregiver acknowledgment program to distinguish representatives who are excellent and recognize their achievements with month to month caregiver grants posted in neighborhood papers.

6. Be industrious in promoting your home care services through networking with nearby specialists, healthcare insurance operators, drug specialists, and elder law lawyers in your locale.

7. Engage individuals at neighborhood temples and caregiver uphold bunches through interest in meetings as they may know others needing your services.

8. Establish common advantageous associations with your rivals by both agreeing to allude clients to each other when an agency cannot offer mentioned types of assistance.

9. Partner with integral businesses, for example, recovery focuses, hospice agencies or a talented home wellbeing agencies. Albeit a hospice or home medical care agency might be providing a day by day attendant or advisor visit there is regularly a hole in close to home care and other help services.

10. Meet with release organizers at nearby clinics and nursing homes to instruct them about your business' non-medical services. Solicitation that social laborers keep your business on record as a referral source when talented care agencies are not suitable.

11. Word of mouth as consistently is the best referral source in your locale. Energize your current and previous clients and caregivers to inform others concerning the quality services your business offers.

12. Lastly understand that numerous families are isolated by separation and frequently go to the internet to investigate home care services. Families seeking caregivers depend on online referrals to assist find with homing care agencies in their loved one's territory.

CHAPTER - 4

UNDERSTANDING SENIORS

Best home care is a confided in asset for providing quality homecare services. By striving to help both client and caregiver, you should comprehend that a sound connection between the two gatherings is fundamental. That is the reason a significant aspect of your central goal must be matching the correct clients with the correct caregivers. Now and then, nonetheless, caregivers may run into a circumstance where a client is being troublesome or putting you in an abnormal condition where you feel vulnerable.

As an expert or family caregiver, you work with various kinds of clients. Some are anything but difficult to coexist with, while others can be a smidgen more troublesome. While this can be frustrating, attempt to recall your client is experiencing numerous dissatisfactions of their own, and you are there to help.

Here are a few different ways you can support these touchier or problematic clients:

Tune in - Maintain eye to eye connection and show that you are listening to what your client needs to state. Manufacture your degree of trust by listening and afterward follow up on what they state.

The most ideal approach to ruin your relationship with clients is to minimize or excuse their issues. When a client begins to mention to you what's up, set aside the effort to listen mindfully. Try not to interject or rationalize, and do not hop directly into an answer. Allow them to finish and attempt to comprehend what they are saying to you. Despite the fact that clients are commonly looking for an answer, being heard is regularly as significant as the arrangement itself. At the point when they finish speaking, express gratitude toward them for confiding in you and rehash back what they said to be certain you comprehend.

Try not to think about it literally - Your client is complaining about an issue, not you. Pull yourself away from the circumstance and find out what is truly going on. Regardless of whether they appear to be attacking you, there is quite often another more profound issue they are vexed about.

Learn as much as possible - To sort out what is happening, you must be eager to pose inquiries. Show your client that you are happy to find out about them and what is going on by taking an opportunity to inquire. Commonly, a client essentially has to realize that you care about them.

Be quite caring - Respond decidedly and be sympathetic. Apologize for any negative insight and make certain to explain the issue. Clients need to see and realize that you care, and it is the best method of saving associations with clients.

Follow up and track the advancement - Write down the entirety of your client's interests and follow up. Inquire as to whether things have improved or not. Note how they improve or diverge and make modifications varying.

In the wake of completing these means, ensure the client is happy with the arrangement and the complaint is settled. In the event that there is as yet an issue, you might need to rehash this cycle until it is sufficiently settled.

Give them you are staying on head of the issue.

Assemble trust - Lack of trust is one of the main reasons' clients can be troublesome, and this can be especially evident when the care provider is new, or where their past care supplier has disregarded their trust in one manner or the other. It is in this manner significant that when dealing with a troublesome client, you give a valiant effort to construct trust and gain proficiency with the propensities and inclinations of your clients. You ought to evaluate your client's circumstance and find out as much about them as possible (without being intrusive or violating their protection). You can interview their loved ones with their authorization to think about your client's preferences, leisure activities, aversions, interests, and character.

That way, you can tailor your care to address their issues and show that you truly care.

Get why – There is an explanation behind each conduct. Your smartest choice is to comprehend why your client carries on in certain manners so you can stay away from those triggers. Some of the time, your client may very well need some rest, now and then they need to be distant from everyone else, now and again their troublesome conduct is a weep for consideration or for somebody to converse with. Different occasions however, honestly, a few clients are simply troublesome, period. Despite the purpose for your client's conduct, it is significant that you abstain from anything that could trigger them into doing things that make your life and caring for them troublesome. In the event that you can put a finger on what sets them off, at that point a large portion of the issue is tackled. The other half is working out how to maintain a strategic distance from such things, and in the occasion, they cannot be dodged, at that point devising an answer and knowing how best to care for them.

Try not to sum up - Some clients misinterpret the least complex things said or see the most innocuous activity with doubt. Again, this could be because of past encounters. Along these lines, when dealing with a troublesome client, you ought to consistently hold up under in mind that your innocent words or activities could trigger negative reactions whenever, and if care is not taken, your relationship with the client can rapidly winding downwards. To dodge such a circumstance, do not expect that every one of your activities are perceived the way you, or every other person, gets them. Continuously recollect that your client is an individual, with their own character. Never, sum up. Come at the situation from their perspective and attempt to comprehend their own view point as opposed to an overall point of view. Search instead for approaches to quiet things down and afterward work from that point to concoct an answer that tends to their complaint (saw or genuine).

Apologize - A sincere conciliatory sentiment is regularly enough to pacify a baffled client. It not just shows you perceive that there is a genuine issue, however it additionally shows that you relate to the client's circumstance and need to transform it. At the point when you apologize, by and by do not rationalize or legitimize the circumstance. Likewise abstain from blaming or criticizing an individual or office. Just state how sorry you are this has occurred and express your longing to help.

Find an answer - Though you may have a snappy answer for the issue, first ask the client what result she or he is hoping for. The appropriate response might be more straightforward than you think. On the off chance that the client's proposal is preposterous, talk about choices until you agree. It is significant that the client is happy with the move you choose to make, so be certain that you both comprehend your strategy.

Act rapidly - Angry customers can be short-intertwined delayed bombs that can make hefty harm an organization's notoriety, so this whole cycle needs to happen rapidly. The entirety of your caregivers and office staff ought to be trained in resolving issues to guarantee that issues are dealt with expeditiously. The more you hold back to react to a complaint, the more noteworthy the difficult will become to the client. When you arrive at an answer, mention to the client what and when you are going to place it into activity and guarantee it seen through.

Maintain A Professional Attitude - While caregivers might be experienced with bad tempered, difficult clients, an expert disposition will conceivably help quiet the nerves of clients and caregivers the same. By understanding that seniors are likely vexed because of feelings based on apparent loss of independence or invasion of protection, caregivers can be understanding and work with clients to cause them to feel as great as conceivable with the circumstance. For instance, a note in your homecare programming or homecare framework regarding a client's absence of solace with help with getting dressed can assist caregivers with facilitating maybe simply laying out garments and letting a client realize they will be directly outside the entryway if help is required. Notwithstanding, homecare programming and homecare frameworks can likewise be used to enable caregivers to impart when clients deny a service or become touchy over certain services.

Work Closely with Family Caregivers to Create an Agreeable Plan of Care - By evaluating what seniors are, and are not happy with by talking with clients, their families, and reviewing notes from caregivers in homecare programming and homecare frameworks, homecare agencies can build up an arrangement of care that will help facilitate the worries of obstinate clients and assist them with feeling calm with the obligations of in-home caregivers.

While homecare is an invaluable asset for some seniors and family caregivers, there will consistently be a few clients who are impervious to change. Notwithstanding, with positive correspondence, care the board and assessment through homecare programming and homecare frameworks, and patient caregivers, even the most reluctant clients can profit by in-home elder care.

Complaints are not charming, but rather negative input is an important piece of development. While complaints are now and again frustrating, they do not need to be damaging on the off chance that you handle them well.

An organization's notoriety is its life blood. A decent notoriety can ensure your clients in the event that you realize how to use it. Shockingly, every organization endures a couple of shots and commits a couple of errors that can harm or even pulverize their notoriety. An investigation by Lee Resources shows that 91% of troubled customers will not willingly work with your organization again. Providers ought to be prepared to deal with these hits, which frequently define whether their organizations will flourish or bite the dust. These basic advances can guarantee that when issues emerge your clients remain cheerful and your notoriety remains intact:

CHAPTER - 5

SENIOR HOMECARE BUSINESS FORMS

A. Explanation of Home Care Services: Comprehensive Home Care Provider

Home Care Provider Name: ____

The following is a rundown of all services that might be given a thorough home care permit.

Each service offered by this provider is indicated by a check in the case close to the service.

☐ Advanced practice nurture services

☐ Registered attendant services

☐ Licensed commonsense medical attendant services

☐ Physical treatment services

☐ Occupational treatment services

☐ Speech-language pathologist services

☐ Respiratory treatment services

☐ Social specialist services

☐ Dietician or nutritionist services

☐ Medication the executives services

☐ Delegated assignments to unlicensed work force

☐ Hands-on help with moves and versatility

☐ Treatment and treatments

☐ Eating help for clients with complicating eating issues (for example trouble swallowing, intermittent lung desires, or requiring the utilization of a cylinder, parenteral or intravenous instruments)

☐ Complex or forte healthcare services

Depict: _________________________ _______________

____

☐ Assistance with dressing, self-feeding, oral cleanliness, hair care, grooming, toileting, and bathing

☐ Standby help within arm's compass for wellbeing while at the same time performing day by day exercises

☐ Verbal or visual reminders to take routinely

planned prescription (includes bringing clients recently set-up drug, drug in original containers, or fluid or on the other hand food to go with the prescription)

☐ Verbal or visual reminders to the client to perform routinely booked medicines what is more, works out

☐ Preparing changed weight control plans requested by a authorized wellbeing proficient

☐ Laundry

☐ Housekeeping/other family tasks

☐ Meal readiness

☐ Shopping

I have gotten a duplicate of this Statement of Home Care Services:

Client Signature: _______________________________ _______ Date: _____

B. Statement of Home Care Services: Basic Home Care Provider

Home Care Provider Name: ___________________ ________________________________

These services could also be given a basic home care license. Each service offered by this provider is indicated by a sign up the box next to the service.

____//

- ☐ Assistance with dressing, self-feeding, oral hygiene, hair care, grooming, toileting, and bathing

- ☐ Standby assistance within arm's reach for safety while performing daily activities

- ☐ Verbal or visual reminders to require regularly scheduled medication

- ☐ Verbal or visual reminders to the client to perform regularly scheduled treatments and exercises

- ☐ Preparing modified diets ordered by a licensed health care provider

- ☐ Laundry

- ☐ Housekeeping/other household chores

- ☐ Meal preparation

- ☐ Shopping

The services listed below are comprehensive home care services and should not be given a basic home care license.

- Advanced practice, registered or licensed practical nurse services

- Physical/occupational therapy, speech-language pathologist or respiratory therapy services

- caseworker, dietician or nutritionist services

- Medication management services

- Delegated tasks to unlicensed personnel

- Hands-on assistance with transfers and mobility

- Treatment and therapies

- Providing eating assistance for clients with complicating eating problems

- Complex or specialty healthcare services

I have received a replica of this Statement of Home Care Services:

Client Signature: _______________________________

Date: _________

CHAPTER - 6

GROWING YOUR BUSINESS

Starting another home care business can be exciting, yet past the energy of being a chief, you have an occupation to develop and sustain your business. As new agencies spring up to serve the aging baby boomer populace, rivalry for this growing business sector will just continue to ascend too.

To rise as a leading agency, you have to set up methodologies that would assist you with staying in the business, yet would empower you get the clients your business needs to develop and thrive.

From customary marketing techniques, for example, attending networking occasions to connecting with possibilities online, you should be both innovative and dynamic to set up a bigger presence in your locale. Verbal exchange will consistently be the best type of marketing your agency, however you essentially cannot depend just on referrals to secure new clients. Have assembled some dependable home care marketing techniques your agency can begin using immediately to take your business to the following level.

- **Set Up Yourself in Your Nearby Network**

One approach to begin in making home care business noticeable is to take an interest in network occasions. Projects and occasions like a run for malignancy, cleaning the network park, or having a corner in a public spot where you can converse with potential clients are typically extraordinary lift to businesses like yours. By getting involved you are saying you care about the network and the individuals in it. Search for chances to get your name out there, and put a face to your organization.

- **Expand Your Advertising**

Attempt to use the same number of channels as your spending will permit to promote your home care business. The objective ought to get your name out there and driving up your notoriety. You could buy announcement space on a road with high traffic, make leaflets that component individuals of various races and sexual orientations, and perhaps place advertisements on the radio when fitting. Make an effort not to put a breaking point on the roads you use so you can connect further.

- **Structure A Partnership with Related Associations**

Try not to fear partnering with other home care agencies that maintain a business in related territories. For instance, on the off chance that you stress standard care, collaborate with an organization that represents considerable authority in Alzheimer's. That way you can allude clients who do not fit under your business to the others and the other way around, enhancing referrals. While you should be certain your businesses are integral, it likewise does not damage to maintain associations with the entirety of your opposition here and there, so you can gather thoughts from their prosperity.

- **Take It to The Internet**

Perhaps the least expensive type of marketing is the online media. In the event that you do not have a business page on Facebook, Twitter, Pinterest and so forth then you have to get one. You have the capability of reaching hundreds, even huge number of individuals just by posting on these locales.

In the event that one individual preference what you post, it is then appeared to their 500 and something companions, and the train continues. In any case, you should be certain you maintain your Facebook page and post to it at any rate week after week, ideally every day. You have to show that your organization is engaging, affable, and alive.

Treat your home care marketing exercises online much like your in-person networking occasions. Zero in on having discussions and getting to know your possibilities as opposed to attempt to offer to them. Pose inquiries, share important information (including your blog entries), and show that you are interested in helping them take care of issues. Web-based media is tied in with building trust with your intended interest group, so remain drew in on the social locales where your possibilities invest the majority of their energy online.

- **Stand Apart from The Competition**

Pinpoint at an opportune time what makes your business stick out, is it the nature of care, insight of caregivers, client fulfillment and so on. Find your trademark, something that the opposition needs, and push that message through the entirety of your correspondence channels. Likewise, offering giveaways and incentives to advance your business consistently helps as well.

- **Build Up A Solid Business Plan**

Volumes have been expounded on writing fruitful business plans, and appropriately too on the grounds that a decent business plan would guarantee that your business remains progressing nicely. Ensure yours includes a diagram of your statement of purpose, marketing technique, hierarchical structure, the board plan, and financial information including fire up expenses and quantifiable profit projections.

- **Request Referrals**

Do you have a client referral program set up? On the off chance that your answer is no, at that point your business could be missing out on an open door for development and you are not alone.

In an ongoing webinar for home care business proprietors, members were overviewed and it was discovered that 67% of them had no client referral program set up.

With a 10.5% higher inquiry to confirmation proportion, for the normal home care business, client referrals could mean an extra gigantic measure of cash in income throughout the following five years. Realize your referral sources and build up a system to get their business. Some conceivable referral sources are;

- specialists (family medicine, cardiology, geriatric medicine, muscular specialists)

- trust officials

- legal counselors

- houses of worship

- senior clubs

- social laborers

- caseworkers

- release organizers

- retirement focuses

- recovery focuses

- supermarkets

- burial service homes

When you recognize your referral sources, build up a contact framework to contact them. Yet, before you begin asking for referrals, you should make client fulfillment your first concern. Your present clients and their families should be very glad and happy with your services.

Their necessities ought to be met, their interests ought to be tended to quickly, and caregivers ought to be trained, inviting and educated. Since your clients interact frequently with your caregivers, it is significant for your caregivers to be glad as well. Glad caregivers lead to cheerful clients. What is more, upbeat clients are well on the way to prescribe your organization to other people.

When you are doing everything, you can to guarantee that your clients are fulfilled, told clients that you value their referrals. Send them cards to distribute to companions or convey reminder letters asking for referrals. Clients may cherish your services, yet they probably will not think to specify it to loved ones. You must get the news out and routinely remind clients to educate everybody regarding your organization.

• **Be Professional**

Your business is basically attending a prospective employee meeting whenever a planned client draws in with you. They can contact you face to face, via telephone, or even by visiting your site, and they have to feel like they can confide in you. Make certain to introduce yourself as caring and solid.

Be prompt in any booked meetings and answer demands right away. It is not remarkable for clients and their families to interface with caregivers through web-based media, so guarantee your group speaks to your organization and its qualities properly through their Facebook pages and other social records. Workers ought to be amenable in dress, way, and discourse.

- **Give Exceptional Customer Service**

Have you ever had a customer contact you just to tell you everything is going impeccably? While this can here and there occur, by far most of customer interactions are solicitations, concerns or complaints. Make certain to fill your customer service positions with the perfect individuals, the individuals who will have tolerance when a troublesome client is being more troublesome than expected.

Training your group to comprehend that they are dealing with genuine individuals who have genuine concerns and needs that must be met can go far in building compassion among your group. Through remarkable customer service, you will fabricate steadfast clients who will at that point prescribe your services to other people.

- **Hotshot Your Upbeat Clients**

No one prefers being the first to a gathering, or anything besides. The music should as of now be playing, individuals ought to move, and everybody ought to yell how wonderful the gathering is. That is the thing that customer tributes accomplish for your home medical care business.

Posting client fulfillment cites on your site and in your handouts comforts your forthcoming customers by showing them how upbeat you make your clients. Pairing these tributes with genuine, proficient evaluation photographs of your clients (not stock photography, however genuine clients) will make this significantly more successful.

- **Be accessible nonstop**

Medical problems do not follow a 9-5 timetable, and actually home care furnishes additional assistance to those with medical problems of some kind. Regardless of whether you have been recruited by the individual you are caring for or by their family, they need you to be accessible whenever.

By making it clear that your group will be accessible nonstop, your clients will have a sense of safety knowing that regardless of what time it is, they can get hold of somebody. On the off chance that you pick not to have an assistant working as the night progressed, you might need to consider forwarding your office's main line to a PDA after normal business hours to answer crisis calls.

- **Screen and Qualify Your Caregivers**

Your caregivers are the essential essence of your business in the field. In this manner, it is essential to enlist qualified caregivers that have experienced an intensive record verification. On the off chance that a man has an aging mother who needs additional care, actually he likely cannot leave his place of employment to deal with her full time. Along these lines, on the off chance that he is going to recruit somebody to be there in his place, you can be certain that he needs somebody who will show his mom the adoration that she merits.

Not every person has the air to be a caregiver, and hiring ought to be finished considering this. This doesn't make them an awful individual; it just methods It is not the proper thing for them. As a home care proprietor, it is your obligation to guarantee your caregivers are qualified and will give the degree of care your clients merit.

- **Market to Your Existing Clients First**

One great approach to advertise a business is to seek your existing clients first for new business before you search out new clients. It costs an agency fivefold the amount of in advertising and marketing between leaflets, promotions, radio, and standard mail to draw in one new client than it accomplishes for an agency to sell added services to an existing client.

The existing client knows your agency, enjoys your agency, and needs to continue doing business with you, so it should take less marketing and advertising dollars to convince that customer to buy extra services from your agency.

- **Practice and Advertise**

It is suggested that all agencies separate themselves by focusing on a specialty market. These can include everything from senior care to home changes to day medical procedure upholds. In the event that you have practical experience in a specific service, gear your home care marketing towards promoting the estimation of the service. For instance, an agency with a senior care strength could contact the applicable or fitting office and inquire as to whether it can publicize with handouts in the waiting room.

- **Build up and Maintain a Reliable Management System**

Clients need to realize that your caregivers will be on schedule, movements will not be disregarded, and that they are being charged reasonably. A powerful homecare programming or homecare framework, combined with educated staff enables your home care business to guarantee clients that no errand is neglected.

By using a homecare programming or homecare framework to log task reminders, just as track caregiver clock-ins and clock-outs at the point-of-care, your agency makes a notoriety for being unfaltering in staying on head of everything about; it is keeping caregivers on schedule, or billing for the right number of hours.

- **Escape the Office Frequently**

Now and then in the beginning of building your business, it is very simple to stall out down and dirty. You are completely overwhelmed by managing the agency and ensuring each undertaking occurs as it must. From answering telephones to handling new clients and talking with their families, to doing finance and training recently recruited employees, your work in the workplace appears to be unending.

While every one of these assignments are significant, it is central you plan time to escape the workplace consistently, also. Up to half of top-notch client introductions originate from home care service providers you meet consistently. Meeting with them oftentimes in person assists work with trusting and guarantee them of the nature of your service.

- **Instruct with Your Blog**

On the off chance that you have not begun a blog on your home care agency's site, you are missing out on one of the most simple and viable approaches to advertise your business online.

Most forthcoming clients research agencies' destinations before making contact, and a blog with instructive substance quite often isolates one agency from another.

Utilize your blog to give valuable information to your intended interest group, for example, tips for better elderly nourishment or how seniors with restricted portability can get more exercise. Become acquainted with the requirements and worries of your possibilities, and afterward compose and post supportive articles consistently.

- **Talk and Write on related issues**

Talk about home care issues at neighborhood gatherings, for example, Rotary, Elks, and senior focuses. Become known as the nearby home care master by appearing on neighborhood syndicated programs to examine ongoing difficulties in the industry. On the off chance that your neighborhood paper has a home care segment, pitch and compose customary visitor articles. On the off chance that it does have one, check whether the manager would include a "Home Care Corner" segment for you to contribute week by week or month to month articles on some issue in home care.

- **Utilize official statements and bulletins**

Compose and disseminate official statements announcing new items, services, or colleagues. Notwithstanding public statements, think about starting a week after week or month to month bulletin to keep in contact with possibilities and clients. Try not to think you have anything new to report every week? However long you are reliably publishing blog entries, you generally have news to impart to everybody on your email list.

- **Hold an Open House**

Network outreach occasions are extremely viable marketing devices for home care agencies. They show your involvement in the network and give phenomenal chances to networking. Sort out an open house at your office once per month or, if your space will not oblige it, contact a neighborhood association, for example, a senior place to have the occasion. Ensure all participants include their email address when they sign your visitor book. You can utilize this contact information to keep in contact with focused interchanges to keep your agency head of-mind.

- **Recognize Your Specialty**

Home care businesses come in numerous assortments, some focusing on more broad care services like housekeeping and friendship, while others worked in intensive live-in care for those suffering from debilitating ongoing conditions. In spite of the fact that more broad types of care are as of now seeing a more popularity, this will change as the Baby Boomer populace ages into their 60s, 70s, and 80s.

- **Sponsorships**

You have to find neighborhood senior occasions that you can help finance through a sponsorship. You recall those enormous pennants on nearby foot races or lager fests? This could be you.

Get your name out there and individuals will say your name. Sponsoring and attending those nearby senior occasions can be fun and loaded with chances to find clients.

- **Host Caregiver Workshops**

Workshops for family caregivers offer an opportunity for care providers to arm themselves with caregiving tips, gain information on maintaining their own wellbeing, and organization with other family caregivers. Work with a neighborhood senior care master, such a doctor or geriatric care supervisor, to support a workshop and gain perceivability with family caregivers in your general vicinity. Consider offering a one-month rebate for caregivers that go to the workshop and attempt your services.

You can similarly begin a caregiver acknowledgment program to distinguish workers who are remarkable and recognize their achievements with month to month caregiver grants posted in nearby papers.

- ### Become a Local Senior Care Advocate

As a business proprietor, make your quality known in the neighborhood senior care field. Work with senior alliances, the nearby senior place and other support gatherings to study the neighborhood senior network. Backer for the wellbeing of current and likely clients, and position yourself as somebody who does not simply give senior care; yet who is enthusiastic about the wellbeing and privileges of our senior populace.

- ### Line up with Disease-Specific Organizations

Visit associations that help with quiet administration of explicit sicknesses. For instance, the American Cancer Society, or ACS, gives information on home care services for territory disease patients. Obtain public accreditation for your agency, as ACS suggests that patients affirm agencies' certifications before considering that agency for home care work.

- ### Partake in Senior Programs

Your city probably offers an assortment of senior residents' projects through the Department of Aging or Senior Services. Visit agency chiefs with information on the services you give and the geographic zone you serve. Circulate limited time materials, for example, a plainly composed leaflet, outlining your services. Finally, inquire as to whether you can have a stall at an upcoming Senior Expo or Senior Center Fair.

Growing your business by implementing each of these means in turn can make your business truly gain speed. Regardless of whether you are not a businessman, you can even now enable your business to develop and stand apart from the opposition, simply step up to the plate and understand that individuals need to work with others. Show your potential clients the sort of individual you are, so they can comprehend from that point the kind of business you run.

CHAPTER - 7

RESOURCES

A great many people do not begin as caregivers knowing the ropes. Unexpectedly, most caregivers will in general learn as they oblige, a decent lot of wrong turns and battles. What helps: knowing where to find solid assistance.

The following associations and experts as assets can assist you with meeting your obligations, cause you to feel less alone, and cut your pressure on the off chance that you are helping a loved senior one who is receiving care at home.

1. Partner Care Services

What they are: Companion care providers do exactly what the name says: give organization to seniors (more seasoned adults), particularly the individuals who are closed ins on account of delicacy or a dementia sickness, (for example, gentle to direct stage Alzheimer's illness, or who live alone. Now and again called "senior friends," these helpers keep a vigilant gaze, apportion day by day prescriptions, drive to hair style appointments, shield somebody flimsy on their feet, perused so anyone might hear, play a card game, plan quick bites and snacks, and in any case work as an additional arrangement of hands, eyes, and feet for your loved one. Buddy care is a growing subset of home care alternatives.

How they help: Companion care is ideal for somebody who might some way or another need to go through aspect of the day alone and who needs some light support. Relatives can work or handle different exercises knowing their loved one is not disregarded. Friend care additionally gives a significant social advantage, decreasing disengagement and improving disposition. Warm connections are regularly shaped when a predictable buddy is at work.

The most effective method to begin: You can find colleagues all alone similarly you would find a babysitter: by talking to neighbors, companions, or relatives, or reaching out to Generation Solutions' senior services coordinator a believed senior care hotspot for more than 20 years. Authorized, reinforced and insured.

2. Individual Care Assistants

What they are: notwithstanding providing friend care, individual care associates offer help with a wide range of exercises of everyday living, from shopping for food to such non-medical individual care as toileting, dressing, grooming, and bathing. They can likewise give impermanent rest care to families.

How they help: Many families enroll individual care partners to tackle issues in their home care circumstance, for example, a little lady hiring a solid helper who can lift a companion for bathing, or a child worried about security hiring a lady to wash his mom. Individual care partners can organize dinner arrangement, escorts to specialist visits, and some other kind of non-medical help your loved one may require in request to live at home longer. In the event that you have to move away for a couple of hours a week or overnight, in-home care can facilitate the concern, particularly if the in-home caregiver is natural to your loved one since the person offers normal types of assistance.

The most effective method to begin: You can find individual care partners all alone by asking companions and neighbors for referrals, or reaching out to Generation Solutions' senior services coordinator a believed senior care hotspot for more than 20 years. Authorized, reinforced and insured.

3. Home Health Agencies

What they are: Home wellbeing agencies are the go-to source when your loved one needs a more elevated level of care, including minor medical care. Affirmed nursing aides have more medical training than elder buddies or individual care partners and should finish tests to get confirmation; they work under a supervising enrolled nurture.

How they help: If your loved one will be released from a medical clinic remain, having somebody around the house who can change wraps or check essential signs can give genuine feelings of serenity. Home wellbeing agencies are once in a while suggested for certain kinds of in-home recovery, for example, exercise-based recuperation. You may likewise invite these services if your loved one needs close to home care or medical care that the family is awkward providing or cannot give, for example, colostomy or wound care, incontinence care, insulin the executives, or other medical services.

Instructions to begin: Talk to your primary care physician on the off chance that you would like to work with a particular home wellbeing agency, or reaching out to Generation Solutions' senior services coordinator a believed senior care hotspot for more than 20 years. Authorized, reinforced and insured.

4. Your neighborhood on Aging

What it is: Your neighborhood on Aging is an administration commanded clearinghouse for general information about close by eldercare services. These agencies offer free referrals to neighborhood services that give transportation, dinners, adult day services, in-home caregivers, legitimate help, home-based training programs for caregivers, and different types of help, all the kinds of services that can assist you with keeping a loved one at home longer. The names of these agencies frequently shift by network. Yet, the services they allude to are generally free or ease, and calling the agency is free.

How it helps: Calls to region agencies on aging are among the best first activities a caregiver can make to gain proficiency with the neighborhood lay of the land on senior care: what kinds of projects, offices, and mastery are accessible in the network. Staff members can address regular inquiries and allude you to assets that are well on the way to coordinate your family's particular needs, speeding your exploration cycle and maybe making you mindful of assets you never knew existed.

Instructions to begin: Contact the staff at your neighborhood on Aging.

5. Geriatric Care Managers

What they are: Geriatric care administrators, or GCMs, survey needs and recognize and coordinate assets for seniors (more established adults). Geriatric care administrators can take over practically all parts of senior care now and again. Some neighborhood government agencies and good cause offer geriatric care consulting services free or on a sliding scale.

How they help: Geriatric care directors are best at helping you sort out care needs when there is an adjustment in circumstance, for example, when your loved one is moving in or has had a wellbeing emergency. They can likewise oversee confounded ongoing care, for example, cases in which various specialists and advisors are involved. Working caregivers and significant distance caregivers find their help financially savvy.

Step by step instructions to begin: Reach out to Generation Solutions' senior services coordinator a believed senior care hotspot for more than 20 years. Authorized, reinforced and insured.

6. Elder law lawyers

What they are: Elder law lawyers will be legal counselors who spend significant time in legitimate and financial issues that are particularly applicable to seniors (more established adults) and to their families including home planning, trusts, and reports to guarantee that medical wishes and financial wishes will be regarded.

How they help: Getting records in request that guarantee your capacity to speak with specialists and banks will streamline your capacity to be a viable supporter and caregiver. Among the authoritative archives your requirement for your loved ones: a development healthcare order, a strong intensity of lawyer for healthcare, a revocable living trust, and a will.

The most effective method to begin: Use Caring.com's Senior Living Directory to look for elder law lawyers by city or postal district and to see ratings and audits.

7. Senior Home Re-modelers

What they are: Senior home re-modelers are developers and home-fix services that represent considerable authority in retrofitting homes to make them protected and open; numerous likewise make new development in view of senior care needs. As a genuinely ongoing subset of the home building industry, they are specialists at assessing peril spots and inconveniences in existing homes, making safe redesigns, (for example, installing snatch bars, widening access for wheelchairs, building inclines), and designing new living spaces. They apply all-inclusive plan principles to make a house you can live in for eternity.

How they help: Whether a loved one is moving in with you or aging set up in their own home, getting an evaluation from a senior home re-modeler is valuable for identifying dated apparatuses and plans that put the individual in danger for falls and different setbacks. Given that an increasing number of families are becoming multi-generational family units, senior home re-modelers can likewise make recommendations for altering an existing structure to give everybody protection.

CHAPTER - 8

HIRING EMPLOYEES

Generally, a specialist is ventured to be a representative aside from in circumstances where the family paying for services can exhibit the laborer's actual independence. Here are the necessary conditions under which a specialist can be viewed as an independent contractual worker, or self-temporary worker, where the business is not liable for finance charge commitments:

The business must have the option to demonstrate that the specialist performs services that the business does not reserve the option to coordinate;

The specialist must maintain an independent business endeavor, including a workspace, outside the business' domain, with his/her own insurance;

The services gave by the laborer are outside the family unit's standard course of business (i.e., work that is distinguished from the everyday activity of the family, for example, woodworkers, roofers, and so on.).

Most senior caregivers who are paid legitimately by the family, or by an outsider installment processor acting in the interest of the family, are representatives, not independent contractual workers. The IRS has instituted new cycles for finding and penalizing managers who inappropriately group a specialist as an independent temporary worker when he is actually a representative.

Steps to Hire an Independent Caregiver

✓   Determining Level of Care/Writing Job Description

Before hiring an independent caregiver, it is critical to determine the degree of care that a loved senior one requires. For instance, take an elderly individual who lives alone and needs friendship, light housecleaning and help with tasks and an individual with Alzheimer's who lives with their adult kid. This individual may require prescription and need broad care five days every week to permit their essential caregiver to work. These two individuals require altogether different degrees of care and care exercises.

When the degree of care has been determined, a set of working responsibilities ought to be composed that is as definite as could reasonably be expected. One will need to include how many hours and days out of every week that care is required and any exceptional aptitudes or training required, for example, involvement in Alzheimer's or dementia care. All obligations the caregiver is to perform ought to be point by point part of the set of working responsibilities. These could include:

- Driving or accompanying the senior to and from appointments

- Running tasks

- Providing oversight and friendship

- Managing medicine

- Assisting with bathing and grooming

- Preparing dinners

- Housecleaning

The individual characteristics one is seeking in a caregiver additionally ought to be secured. For example, a patient individual with a merry, energetic character.

✓ **Determining Pay Rate**

There are two factors that go into determining the compensation rate for independent caregivers: government law and nearby market pricing.

Depending on the locale of the US, families ought to hope to pay independent caregivers between $10 - $20 every hour.

Independent caregivers are viewed as family unit representatives, and family unit workers are considered non-excluded workers. This implies they are dependent upon the Fair Labor Standards Act (FLSA) guidelines. The FLSA is a government law that sets the minimum compensation, just as expects additional time to be paid for the individuals who work more than 40 hours/week.

✓   **Relatives Or Related Caregivers Are Not Excluded From This Law**

Territorial monetary factors extraordinarily sway the hourly rate independent caregivers are paid. In only a couple of disengaged zones, caregivers make minimum pay. In many areas, independent caregivers are paid between $10 - $20 every hour. The normal hourly rate for home care agencies is accessible here. Independent caregivers are regularly paid 30% not exactly home care agencies.

✓   **Finding and Interviewing a Caregiver**

There are numerous roads wherein one can find an independent caregiver. Ask companions, neighbors, senior focuses, temples, the senior's essential specialist, and social laborers on the off chance that they know a senior caregiver who is looking for work. Search and/or post the situation on online employment sheets or look or spot an advertisement in the grouped segment of your neighborhood paper. Another extraordinary asset is to contact your neighborhood on Aging (AAA), and inquire as to whether they are aware of any senior caregivers in the region in which you live.

An initial interview via telephone can help tight down candidates before interviewing face to face. This can be kept basic and include the rudiments, for example, the hours/days one is relied upon to work, explicit caregiving obligations, and approaches to be followed, as not smoking in the house. The subsequent stage would be face to face interviews and are more inside and out. Ask candidates a lot of inquiries and spread themes, for example,

- Past work insight

- Training/exceptional aptitudes

- What they have loved/disdained about past positions

- How they would deal with a troublesome care beneficiary

- What they like about working with seniors

- Finally, have them meet the individual for whom they will give care.

✓ Conducting a Background Check

When a caregiver has been picked, a historical verification is significant. A record verification may include the following:

- Confirming earlier business

- Checking references

- Verifying affirmations/licenses

- Doing a criminal individual verification

- Checking credit reports

- Obtaining DMV records

There are a few manners by which one can have an individual verification directed. For instance, one may experience a law office or a private investigator, as they frequently have specific information bases, allowing them to do historical verifications. One may likewise select to experience an online organization, which is commonly more moderate (hope to pay under $100). Make note, officially, one needs a marked delivery from the possible caregiver in request to play out a personal investigation.

✓ Creating an Independent Caregiver Contract

When an independent caregiver has been recruited, work contract (otherwise called a business contract) should be agreed upon. This is a composed understanding, and ought to include the following:

- Start date of business

- Desires

- Installment sum

- Excursion days

Obligations the caregiver is to perform

This is a significant method to secure oneself as a business in the occasion questions emerge about what the activity involves. A case of an independent caregiver contract understanding can be found here. The caregiver should sign two duplicates, one for the caregiver and one for the business.

For the most part, a senior home care specialist who is recruited to care for the everyday needs of an aging adult is a worker. All things considered, the business, either the family or the agency, is liable for work charges, record keeping and required insurance matters. This is valid for most senior caregivers you recruit secretly, and furthermore those senior caregivers you enlist with the help of a vault service who may encourage installments however is not the business.

5 Benefits of Hiring in Home Caregivers

There are relatively few things that can turn your life around like a relative losing physical or mental abilities. A few people frequently think the main choice is sending your beloved relative into a recovery place or a nursing home. That isn't your solitary choice. In home caregivers can offer types of assistance to assist your loved one continue with living at home.

In home care for seniors is an extraordinary method to guarantee your loved one is being cared for appropriately. For when you can't be there, 24-hour home care has numerous advantages.

Here are a couple to consider

1. Staying in the solaces of home

One of the most appealing advantages of senior care is that your loved one will have the option to remain in their home. Almost 90% of seniors need to remain in their own homes as they age since it accompanies the capacity to live under one's own principles. For 42% of seniors participating in home care, making their own guidelines is a key purpose behind choosing senior care.

2. Customized care

You can have confidence that your loved one

will get particular, one on one care when you have an assistant gone to the house. They will not get this quality 24-hour home care on the off chance that they moved into a nursing home, so this technique will assist them with achieving extreme solace.

3. Your true serenity

Worrying about your parent each day is no simple assignment. The most ideal approach to guarantee your own true serenity with regards to their care is to employ an expert helper who can give a scope of care.

4. They can even now partake in the exercises they love

Does your loved one appreciate spending time in their nursery, or walking their canine around the square? On the off chance that they remain in their home, they can at present do these exercises with the assistance of a helper. Also, the most joyful of retirees are the individuals who are occupied with three to four exercises routinely, so their happiness will rely on it.

5. Their personal satisfaction will be improved

At the point when you utilize a caregiver into your loved one's home, their battles will be promptly lifted. The objective of the caregiver is to make their life more straightforward in any manner conceivable. They will likewise feel quieter and more loosened up knowing they don't need to stress over handling regular things without anyone else.

6. Transportation

One of the most widely recognized difficulties of growing old is the possible inability to drive because of changes in vision (helpless sight), loss of capacity or pain from driving. Home caregivers can ship aging adults to and from significant medical, stores, social visits and different tasks, eliminating the need to depend on open transportation and ensuring seniors can go to significant appointments.

In home caregivers comprehend that there are still things you have to complete consistently, paying little heed to your age.

7. Minds Wellbeing

Having a loved one age set up can be challenging, particularly on the off chance that you happen to live out of state. Home care organizations can perform ordinary wellbeing checks to guarantee seniors have satisfactory food, utilitarian heating and cooling, and the capacity to deal with their drugs. On the off chance that you live far away from your loved one, these visits can furnish you with genuine feelings of serenity.

8. Great Nutrition

Seniors and their families ought to keep in mind the estimation of dinner arrangement services. Numerous seniors depend on cheap food, solidified dinners, and other low-esteem, readymade nourishments for sustenance. In-home caregivers can give new, supplement rich nourishments that help ideal wellbeing and higher energy levels.

Certain age-related conditions can make it all the more challenging for seniors to age set up securely and easily, however the live-in care specialists are accessible nonstop to assist seniors with managing their wellbeing. Regardless of whether your loved one is living with dementia or is recovering from a stroke; you can trust in proficient live-in caregivers to upgrade their personal satisfaction.

9. No Need to Lose Your Independence

At the point when you begin to live in a nursing home, it is entirely expected to feel lost your independence. Numerous individuals choose to move into a nursing home, in light of the fact that there are a few things that they cannot achieve at home alone. Nursing homes offer medical help and help with things that you probably will not have the option to do all alone, yet you need to live with them to accomplish it. At-home caregivers permit you get the chance to get help in the solace of your own home.

10. Help around the House

In your more seasoned years, it turns out to be harder to complete basic errands such a cooking for yourself, cleaning up around the house, doing clothing, and taking garments to the laundry. With the assistance of an at home caregiver, things like light housekeeping services are finished for you. They can assist you with completing your clothing and different errands while additionally providing you with dinner readiness services. There is no compelling reason to pressure any longer about how you will complete things.

11. Private Attention

At nursing homes, it is not exceptional for the workers to disregard your own needs. With an at home care provider, you will be given the private consideration that you merit. Your needs and needs will consistently be thought of and dealt with easily.

12. Customized Meals

As a rule, nursing home dinners are like a cafeteria in an evaluation school. They have a timetable with explicit dinners every day. After some time, it can turn out to be so unremarkable to eat something very similar again and again, particularly on the off chance that you do not care for it. Home caregivers can cook for you, and utilize the ingredients that you want.

FREQUENTLY ASKED QUESTIONS ON SENIOR HOME CARE BUSINESS

Straightforwardness is essential to us. Starting a senior home care business must be an ideal choice for you, so we need you to have everything the information you require to settle on an informed choice about pursuing subsequent stages.

1. How before long would you be able to put a caregiver?

We can put a Caregiver when you need one. We should simply evaluate your circumstance, get an understanding of your needs, and afterward coordinate you with a Caregiver who can be there for you on the very beginning. For those occasions when sudden circumstances introduce themselves, we have our Rapid Care Response framework for fast service.

2. Are your caregivers insured?

All Home Helpers Home Care Caregivers are insured and needed to go through an intensive individual verification. They are additionally appropriately screened to guarantee your loved one and their homes are completely ensured.

3. Does your in-home care agency direct historical verifications on your representatives?

Truly, every one of our Caregivers must pass a broad historical verification to work for our organization.

4. Are your caregivers trained to deal with extreme clients? What kind of training and continuing instruction does this in-home care agency give to your caregivers?

At Home Helpers Home Care, our Caregivers are trained to deal with anything. Our nitty gritty training educational program and ongoing training ensure they are in every case completely set up to care for their clients. We additionally offer our Home Helpers University, which not just gives ongoing training through courses and webinars, however offers our Caregivers the chance to acquire confirmations of Specialist, Expert, and Master, every one of which separates the ranges of abilities of every one of our staff.

5. On the off chance that the caregiver does not work out, what do you do to find a substitution?

Home Helpers Home Care consistently needs to ensure that the Caregiver we place with your loved one is the most ideal counterpart for their circumstance and their needs. On the off chance that they are not as viable as we trusted, we will rapidly attempt to put another one in your home.

6. Who would it be a good idea for me to contact with inquiries concerning my caregiver?

Just contact your nearby Home Helpers Home Care agency to talk with either an Office Manager or a Supervisor. We will rapidly address any inquiries or concerns you may have.

7. Do I pay the caregiver legitimately, or do I tip the caregiver?

No, you don't pay your Caregiver straightforwardly, and they are not permitted to acknowledge tips. You will pay your Home Helpers Home Care agency straightforwardly. We acknowledge most techniques for installment and the hourly rates for our Caregivers will change depending on the spot. Every one of our agencies is privately possessed and worked, which is the reason hourly rates will vary starting with one area then onto the next.

8. Imagine a scenario where my caregiver does not appear for a planned move.

Despite the fact that this is an exceptionally uncommon occasion that we do not anticipate happening, if your Caregiver does not appear, we will be alarmed right away. We use a framework that permits Caregivers to check in and out, so on the off chance that they do not check in, our agency will quickly be told. This framework additionally eliminates the requirement for timesheets and minimizes missed movements.

9. Who will I meet at the initial in-home care appraisal?

In spite of the fact that it shifts starting with one area then onto the next, you will undoubtedly meet the proprietor, enlisted medical attendant, or client care director (or a combination). On the off chance that you are prepared to find home care currently, plan your evaluation today.

10. How would you find and select quality caregivers?

Home Helpers Home Care has a few solid recruiting strategies for finding new Caregivers. We use sites, target gatherings, work fairs, and centered advertising. We at that point put interested candidates through an exhaustive interview measure that includes both individual and gathering settings.

11. Would i be able to converse with any of your present clients?

Indeed! This is an incredible method of trying to choose if you have settled on a decent decision in trusting a home care agency, and our agency will have the option to place you in contact with current clients.

12. How would I find customers?

Since there is such an interest for good home care providers, you simply need to tell prospects that you are accessible. There are twelve neighborhood wellsprings of free referrals recorded in my book. The best wellspring of new clients, obviously, is informal exchange from fulfilled clients. At the point when you are first starting out, leave a couple of business cards and flyers or pamphlets at the neighborhood senior focus and run a free promotion.

13. How frequently are your in-home care services accessible?

Our services are altered to address your issues. Regardless of whether you need us for a couple of hours seven days, a couple of hours daily, or day in and day out, we will structure our care intend to accommodate your necessities. This will be talked about during your free In-Home Care Assessment.

14. What services do you give?

We give a wide scope of services. Look at our Services page to find out more and afterward contact your nearby agency for additional subtleties and to find home care now.

15. Is it costly to begin?

Not in the slightest degree. All you truly need is transportation, which in many territories implies a solid vehicle. In numerous urban communities, it is simpler to utilize public transportation due to parking and traffic issues. Obviously, you will require a cellphone to keep in contact with clients and possibilities. Some other things required by a particular client would be given by and paid to by the client or their family. At the point when you are starting out, you will require business cards and flyers or leaflets, however that is a little cost, generally under $300.

16. Do you truly care about my family and I?

For more than 20 years, we have been proving to our customers that their wellbeing, security, and solace are our main need. So truly, we certainly care about helping you and your family.

17. Is this a sans smoke home care agency?

Each agency is independently claimed and worked, yet a considerable lot of our workplaces are without smoke. You can call your neighborhood agency to twofold check.

18. What is Caring OnDemand?

Caring OnDemand is a home care service and innovation stage that associates you to a cross country organization of confirmed home care providers you can employ day and night.

19. What represents the fast development of the business?

Home care services are the quickest developing aspect of the whole medical care industry in America. Indeed, the U.S. Division of Labor says non-medical home caregivers are the most popular activity now, and likely for the following twenty years. There are two explanations behind this interest. To begin with, medical advances have caused it feasible for individuals to be cared for at home as opposed to in a clinic or nursing home. Second, increasing expenses of medical services have made a growing interest for more moderate in-home care.

20. For what reason would it be a good idea for me to utilize Caring OnDemand?

Did you know one of the main expenses of home care is the time a caregiver sits and holds up in the middle of undertakings?

Caring OnDemand is the main homecare service without hourly minimums, so you or a loved one can get care for just insofar as required.

21. Does somebody diverse go to my home each time? Imagine a scenario where I like a particular caregiver.

We urge every one of our clients to frame bonds with caregivers. This makes for a more charming encounter for both you and the caregiver. Thus, in the event that you have a unique bond with a caregiver, you are allowed to demand their services or set up a recurring visit from them. A consistency in care encourages caregivers to see any adjustments in your condition that ought to be imparted to your family or a medical expert. It likewise causes you assemble trust in their abilities and their character.

Notwithstanding, we should take note of that in the event that you do not have a recurring visit from a particular caregiver, they may not be accessible at the specific time you need them. All things considered; we will dole out one of the numerous other qualified caregivers.

22. Would i be able to meet the home care provider before I start service?

Truly! Caring OnDemand offers a free health appraisal visit preceding starting care. You just timetable this conference, and an agency delegate will meet with you in your home. During this visit, the delegate will bring an understanding for you to sign and furthermore build up a fundamental care plan and timetable planned explicitly for your necessities. They can likewise tell you the best way to utilize innovation to plan visits and deal with your record.

To begin, either demand a free counsel visit by means of the application, or call us at Caring OnDemand. We would be more than willing to plan a period for you to meet your care group.

23. Do I need to pay with a charge or Visa?

At the point when you pursue a record with Caring OnDemand, you are needed to input a check card or Visa number. While we don't acknowledge money of check installment for homecare, you can change the charge or Mastercard you're using whenever. There are several reasons why we just acknowledge advanced installment. To start with, it assists caregivers with avoiding the weight of carrying installments around or transporting them to the agency. Likewise, this permits you to get to your whole installment history online, which minimizes administrative work and invoices for the caregiver, the agency the caregiver works for, and obviously, you and your family.

24. I do not have a cell phone. Would i be able to in any case utilize Caring OnDemand?

In the event that you do not have a cell phone, do not stress. There are a lot of different ways you can at present utilize and profit by Caring OnDemand. To begin with, you can get to our site using your computer or work station. You can do any of the required scheduling or record alters online that you would somehow or another do on the application.

You can converse with your relatives and check whether somebody would download the Caring OnDemand application on their telephone and timetable visits for you. On the off chance that you pick this alternative, you ought to guarantee you pick somebody who is regularly accessible, since you don't generally have a clue when you will require care. On the off chance that your child is the person who timetables visits for you, yet he takes some time off, he might be delayed to react, and accordingly, you may be waiting quite a while for care.

Finally, you can simply get the telephone and call us. At Caring OnDemand, we need to make the way toward securing care as simple as could be expected under the circumstances, and we are glad to assist you with scheduling any care visits you need via telephone.

25. Imagine a scenario in which there is more than one senior in a family.

On the off chance that both you and your companion actually live in your home or you live with a sibling or companion that likewise needs care, you can both profit by homecare services. Remember that this will mean more work for the caregiver, so plan for an increase in time and cost.

26. Am I qualified for Home Care services?

It would be ideal if you see Your Guide to Home Care Services in Manitoba.

27. Who recruits senior home care providers?

Senior care experts, for example, release organizers at neighborhood medical clinics and assisted-living offices are continually looking for proficient, solid home caregivers. Adult offspring of seniors who need in-home care are a prime wellspring of new clients too. A large number of them utilize the internet to look for a caregiver, so it is a smart thought to enlist with at least one of the online care provider referral services.

28. What is the contrast between in-home medical care and non-medical home care?

In home medical services requires medically trained medical services laborers, for example, attendants. Non-medical care involves just the assignments that do not need medical training. For instance, a non-medical home care provider can remind a client to take their meds, yet cannot administer the meds.

29. What Home Care services are accessible?

It would be ideal if you see Your Guide to Home Care Services in Manitoba.

30. I am moving my family to another province. One of my relatives needs home care. How would I approach getting them home care services in our new area?

You should contact the neighborhood wellbeing expert in the province or region you are moving to, and examine the particular circumstance. Every province has somewhat extraordinary Home Care qualification rules, services accessible and financial courses of action. Provinces likewise have distinctive waiting periods until people moving to their province are qualified for service.

31. Who will pay for Home Care until my relative is qualified for services in the other province?

Manitoba does not pay for Home Care services once an individual move from the province. Individuals should check any strengthening health care coverage inclusion they may have and ought to likewise investigate any exceptions to waiting periods in different provinces/domains.

Individuals may likewise need to pay for services in different provinces that were given without charge to the client when they were in Manitoba.

Home Care is not an insured advantage secured under the arrangements of the Canada Health Act.

In the event that qualified, inclusion will begin on the main day of the third month after appearance in Manitoba. When inclusion in Manitoba begins, home care services might be gotten to by contacting the local wellbeing authority of habitation. The provincial home care program will at that point coordinate the appraisal cycle needed to initiate services.

Individuals who got home care services in their past home ward may wish to contact the territorial home care program upon appearance to Manitoba to help with the change. Note that individuals may incur an expense for services during the sit tight period for Manitoba Health inclusion.

32. What amount are senior home caregivers paid?

There is a major distinction in the compensation for caregivers who work for a home care agency and the individuals who have their own independent home care service. For instance, an agency may charge the client $24 60 minutes, however just compensation the caregiver $12

60 minutes. That is the reason it is ideal to be an independent caregiver, with your own business name, so you can get the best rates in your general vicinity. On the off chance that you are getting paid $12 60 minutes, you will make just $24,000 per year. As an independent caregiver, doing a similar work, you will have the option to charge $24, and make $48,000 per year. Which would you rather win $24,000 or $48,000?

33. I need to fire up my own Home Care business. What are the licensing necessities from Manitoba Health, Seniors and Active Living?

Manitoba Health, Seniors and Active Living does not permit private Home Care organizations or agencies. These organizations must meet a similar business licensing and work principles as some other organization being set up.

34. What does a senior home care provider do?

Most senior home care clients are somewhere in the range of 65 and 95 years of age, living in their own home, who simply need assistance with day by day living exercises, for example, clothing, supper readiness, housekeeping and drug reminders. A home care provider causes them live at home by taking care of these assignments, and furthermore give friendship by listening to their clients, reading a book to them or playing cards.

35. Are relatives qualified to be paid for nonprofessional services which would somehow or another be given by Home Care?

Manitobans might be qualified to be paid for home care services they give to relatives through Self and Family Managed Care. Qualification of a relative for installment must be determined by the territorial wellbeing authority before the relative can get installments for nonprofessional services that Home Care would some way or another give.

In November 2009, Manitoba Health, Seniors and Active Living amended the provincial approach that outlines when an individual can be paid for providing home care nonprofessional services to a relative. For more information and the qualification necessities, if you don't mind contact your neighborhood provincial wellbeing authority.

36. Would i be able to work low maintenance?

Truly, in many instances you can. You can tailor your work routine to fill in so much or as meager as you need to permit you time for different things, for example, family duties. Most non-medical home care clients just require 3-4 hours of the day, so you could work half-days, for instance.

37. Imagine a scenario where I have never done this.

Non-medical in-home care is not advanced science, so in the event that you have fundamental housekeeping abilities, you will do fine and dandy. In the event that you are uncertain of yourself, go to work for a home care agency for half a month to realize what is expected to work superbly. On the off chance that you are a caring individual and a decent audience, you will progress admirably.

38. Do I need any uncommon training or a declaration?

Except if you intend to offer home medical care services, which would require medical training, there are no class necessities or confirmation. In certain territories, the Red Cross offers home care classes, and a couple of junior colleges additionally have programs. In spite of the fact that there are at present no proper training necessities, you should attempt to study your work, and maybe even consider getting a CNA declaration. That training will assist you with doing a superior activity for clients, and permit you to charge a smidgen more for your services.

39. Would i be able to utilize both home care and home wellbeing?

Indeed! Home wellbeing and home care can be utilized at the same time. Truth be told, home care is regularly used to help and supplement the care gave by home wellbeing. For instance, the home wellbeing attendant can set up prescriptions, and your caregiver can remind you to take them.

Way of life Options conveys both home care and home nursing permit, which implies we can likewise give a portion of similar nursing services offered through home wellbeing, varying.

40. When is the best an ideal opportunity to set up home care or geriatric care the board services?

A great many people do not begin researching or coordinating these services until the need is intense. Shockingly, this can leave you scrambling to find assets finally. Preferably, you should begin making home care courses of action when the exercises of everyday living originally become challenging. With appropriate care, more established adults can remain independent at home longer.

Home care is likewise a supportive choice for those that have as of late been released from the medical clinic, recovery focus or long-haul care office, ensuring that necessities are met during the basic recuperation measure.

41. How frequently are home wellbeing services given?

Home wellbeing needs are determined by the doctor, and the services gave and recurrence of care relies upon the arrangement of care coordinated by your doctor.

Home care then again taxi be planned whenever the timing is ideal as regularly as care is required.

42. When might I utilize a geriatric care director?

Geriatric care the executive's services are useful for more established adults without youngsters, those with family who live out of the territory, or those whose wards cannot aid the administration of their care. It is likewise an incredible alternative when care needs are mind boggling and additionally numerous assets are expected to oversee care.

43. Would i be able to set aside cash by using a private caregiver?

Hiring a private caregiver may appear to be a

less exorbitant option in contrast to a private obligation agency, nonetheless, its transporters a far more serious danger than a great many people figure it out. From insurance obligation to charges, it is imperative to teach yourself on the dangers of hiring a private, unlicensed caregiver.

SOME EXTRA TIPS

A. Home care services for seniors

Need to age set up? Find out about home care services that can assist you with maintaining your independence and remain at home for more.

What are home care services for seniors?

While it might be difficult to acknowledge, a large portion of us will require some kind of care help after the age of 65. You might be accustomed to handling everything yourself, dividing up obligations with your mate, or relying on relatives for minor assistance around the home. In any case, as you get more established and your conditions change, getting around and taking care of yourself can turn out to be increasingly troublesome. On the off chance that moving to a retirement network, assisted living office, or nursing home does not advance, home care services might have the option to help keep you living in your own home for more.

Home care services include:

Family unit maintenance. Keeping a family unit running easily takes a great deal of work. In the event that you are finding it difficult to keep up, you can investigate clothing, shopping, gardening, housekeeping, and jack of all trade's services. In the event that you are having inconvenience staying on head of bills and appointments, financial and healthcare the executives may likewise be useful.

Transportation - Transportation is a major question for more established adults. Perhaps you are finding it difficult to drive or do not care to drive around evening time. Having admittance to trains, transports, rideshare applications, diminished charge cabs, and senior transportation services can help delay your independence and maintain your interpersonal organization.

Home alterations - On the off chance that your portability is becoming restricted, home changes can go far towards keeping your existing home agreeable and available.

Alterations can include things, for example, snatch bars in the shower, inclines to evade or minimize the utilization of steps, or in any event, installing another restroom on the ground floor.

Individual care - Help with the exercises of everyday living, for example, dressing, bathing, or supper readiness, is called individual or custodial care. Home wellbeing helpers can give individual care services that extend from a couple of hours daily to nonstop live-in care. They may likewise give restricted help things, for example, taking circulatory strain or offering prescription reminders.

Medical care - Some healthcare services can be given at home via trained experts, for example, word related advisors, social specialists, or home wellbeing attendants. Check with your insurance or wellbeing service to perceive what kind of inclusion is accessible, in spite of the fact that you may need to take care of some expense using cash on hand. Hospice care can likewise be given at home.

Day programs - Day projects or adult daycare can assist you with keeping occupied with exercises and socialization during the day, while providing a break for your caregivers. Some daycare programs are essentially social, while others give restricted wellbeing services or represent considerable authority in problems, for example, beginning phase Alzheimer's.

B. Is aging set up ideal for you?

It is normal to need to remain at home as you become more seasoned. The natural can be comforting as we face the misfortunes that inevitably accompany aging, and your home is likely loaded up with affectionate recollections and your neighborhood with recognizable individuals. Be that as it may, taking a stage back to take a gander at the master plan can assist you with deciding whether staying at home for the long haul genuinely is the correct advance for you. Over and over again, choices to venture out from home are made unexpectedly after an abrupt misfortune or wellbeing emergency, making modifications even more painful and troublesome. Prior planning and examining which home care services are accessible can settle on it simpler to settle on the decision that is appropriate for both you and your family.

Obviously, everybody's needs differ, depending on components, for example, how much help you have, your overall wellbeing and versatility, and your financial circumstance. Here are a portion of the issues to consider while evaluating your aging set up and home care alternatives:

Area and availability - Where is your home found? Is it accurate to say that you are in a provincial or rural zone that requires a ton of driving? In the event that you are in a territory with more open travel, is it safe and effectively available? What amount of time does it require for you to get to services, for example, shopping or medical appointments? It is likewise critical to consider nearness to network services and exercises.

Home openness and maintenance - Is your home effectively adjusted? Does it have a great deal of steps or a lofty slope to get to? Do you have an enormous yard that should be maintained?

Backing accessible - Do you have loved ones close by? How involved would they say they are? Is it accurate to say that they are ready to give you the help you need? Numerous more established adults like to depend on family to give assistance, however as your needs increase, they probably will not have the option to fill in the entirety of the holes. Caregiving can be truly and genuinely exhausting, particularly on the off chance that it is basically on one individual, for example, a companion or youngster. Your connections might be more beneficial on the off chance that you are available to getting help from more than one source.

Seclusion - In the event that it gets troublesome or inconceivable for you to venture out from home without assistance, separation can quickly set in. You will most likely be unable to take an interest in leisure activities you once loved, remain involved in network service that kept you persuaded, or visit with loved ones. Losing these associations and backing is a formula for despondency.

Medical conditions - Nobody can foresee what is to come. Nonetheless, on the off chance that you or your mate has a constant medical condition that is required to exacerbate after some time, it is particularly imperative to think about how you will deal with wellbeing and versatility issues. What are regular intricacies of your condition, and by what method will you handle them?

Finances - Making a financial plan with foreseen costs can assist you with weighing the upsides and downsides of your circumstance. Substitute game plans like assisted living can be costly, however broad in-home assistance can quickly get costly also, particularly at more significant levels of care and live-in or 24-hour inclusion.

Your family's opinions - Normally, you have the final choice with respect to where you need to live, yet input from relatives can be useful. Is it true that they are stressed over your wellbeing or a medical issue that will inevitably require hefty care? Listening to concerns and keeping a receptive outlook are critical.

C. Motivations to invest in a home care business

In the event that you are prepared for your

next enormous move however do not need the pressure that accompanies starting a whole new business without any preparation, purchasing an existing business or an establishment can be an extraordinary choice. The uplifting news: there are numerous alternatives to browse. The nearly as-uplifting news: there are endless choices to browse. On the off chance that you are looking for a chance to construct your own business and have a beneficial outcome in your locale, a home care business may be an incredible fit.

1. It is an industry with 'heart'

This is your opportunity to genuinely have any kind of effect in individuals' lives, regardless of whether you are working with clients, caregivers, or families. You could possess an inexpensive food joint, yet it is not probably going to give you similar feeling of satisfaction as helping individuals in your locale with home care.

2. Interest for home care is growing (without any indications of slowing!)

Baby Boomers are currently hitting their 60s and 70s. Within the following not many years, we are going to see a spike in the aging populace, just as in the senior care industry.

Numerous seniors would want to remain at home as long as truly conceivable, instead of experience their more established a long time in a care office. Presently is the ideal chance to get set up for the home care boom, and help Boomers serenely acclimate to aging at home.

3. You need not bother with a medical services foundation

While a foundation in medical services is a definite resource, senior care is the ideal choice for any individual who flourishes with making individuals glad. On the off chance that you are new to the industry, it merits asking the specialists to allude you to the best assets and give tips to determine if this following stage is appropriate for you.

4. Home care is a downturn versatile industry

In the event that there is one thing that is becoming increasingly apparent during the current financial atmosphere, it is that home care really is a downturn tough industry. As the impression of home care continues to move and it is no longer observed as an untimely idea, request continues to develop while different industries might be confronted with ongoing difficulties. Coronavirus and financial uncertainty aside, individuals will at present continue to age and seniors are as yet going to require care in the solace of their own homes.

5. It is the ideal decision for individuals who love individuals

Home care definitely is not solo work, the very definition involves assisting others. In the event that you love being encircled by other people who love making a distinction, home care might just be your next calling. Business ought to be about something other than the reality, and home care is an extraordinary method to combine benefit with reason.

6. It is a chance to draw nearer to the network

As an 'extrovert', having a senior care business can give you one more motivation to interact with your locale. Not exclusively are verbal exchange and individual to-individual interactions significant marketing instruments in this industry, giving back and getting involved can feel similarly in the same class as the work you will do. On the off chance that you collaborate with a brand like Nurse Next Door who can deal with the scheduling solicitations of your clients and caregivers, you will have the opportunity to chip in at nearby occasions and become more acquainted with the network better.

7. You will not need to sit behind a work area throughout the day

You will experience individuals in a wide range

of conditions: at home, at the workplace, at medical offices, and even at occasions. You can pick your degree of in-person involvement, which settles on home care an extraordinary decision for those looking for an adaptable way of life.

8. The Home care industry is enormous

Home care is a 93-billion-dollar industry (US) and is growing quickly. Studies venture the quantity of Americans 65+ will twofold by 2050, and it is normal that 66% of that age gathering will require long haul care in the course of their life. This is the place it assists with thinking long haul. Jumping on board presently implies that you will have the option to build up your home care business before there is a boom in senior care providers, as well.

9. You will meet other reason driven individuals

Your viewpoint will have a gigantic effect on your clients' insight. In the event that you consider aging to be despairing and solemn, you will pass those feelings to your group and your clients.

In any case, on the off chance that you are in it to assist individuals with aging more joyful and feel good, your feelings will stream down through each degree of your business. The individuals you recruit will be similarly as reason driven as you, and you will quickly encounter the prizes that originate from having a positive group. Another advantage of buying a home medical care establishment is that you will get the opportunity to gain from other energetic franchisees who feel similarly tantamount to you do about providing extraordinary service to individuals needing in-home help.

10. Home medical care is digging in for the long haul

In the event that you were getting on in age and needing help, okay want to be at home with a caregiver, or in a medical clinic? You would probably pick the previous. Numerous individuals feel the equivalent, and that is not going to change at any point in the near future.

It is an extraordinary opportunity to get into home care, the need is going to drastically increase throughout the following not many years as Baby Boomers hit their 80s, and it is likely going to continue for an additional 20 years. Reports show that the industry is set to encounter quick development, and it is uncommon to have the option to figure an impending movement like this.

Make the most of the chance and get into the home medical care business now!

CONCLUSION

Home care help services can turn into a significant and integral aspect of your life as you step through your brilliant years and plan the following stages for your most current excursion, energy, interest, or objective. With endless agencies accessible available today, it very well may be hard to settle on the correct decision.

Notwithstanding, with a sharp eye on perspectives, for example, polished methodology, compassion, notoriety, and that's only the tip of the iceberg, you can make the important strides and quick exploration involved to handily recognize the best service for your interesting and individual needs.

Providing you with the degree of help you require and a recurrence you like, home cares are invaluable assets that let you center around becoming the most advantageous and most powerful form of yourself ever with a day to day existence loaded with confidence, soul, elegance, excitement, and, in particular, quality.

On the off chance that you show at least a bit of kindness for caring, this is the ideal opportunity to have any kind of effect in how individuals live. Invest with reason in a set up business model that your locale will welcome. This is your opportunity to become familiar with home care establishment proprietorship and set yourself on the correct way for your future.